Stories that Explain

Social stories for children with autism in primary school

Lynn McCann

Permission to photocopy

Stories that Explain

ISBN: 978-1-85503-618-5

© Lynn McCann 2018

Illustration © Robin Lawrie

This edition published 2018

10 9 8

Printed in the UK by Page Bros Ltd, Norwich

Designed and typeset by Andy Wilson for Green Desert Ltd

LDA, 2 Gregory Street, Hyde, Cheshire SK14 4HR

www.ldalearning.com

Contents

CD-ROM Contents

Introduction

Autistic children can find the world a confusing place. They will have an autistic way of perceiving the world that can be different from people who are not autistic (neurotypical people or NT's), and this impacts the way they interact with other people and the social world around them. Schools are very social places. The social demands on children start the moment they walk through the school gate and continue relentlessly throughout the day until they leave at 3.15 pm. Parents will then have to deal with a child who is exhausted and overwhelmed just through having to use so much energy in interacting socially all day. There are then additional social demands from family interactions, such as being out in the community, appointments and celebration events.

Autistic children and adults can find it difficult to understand the perspectives of other people in a social situation and struggle to know how to act and react to their socially different peers. Most children with autism are keen to have positive social interactions — they want to enjoy being with others. Much of the help they need is simply understanding and approaches from others that take into account how they perceive the world. Part of the support we can give autistic children is to explain different perspectives in a way they can understand and help them to develop a wider view of the situations that they find confusing. We can also explain the autistic perspective to neurotypical children. It works both ways.

The effort others put into communicating effectively and accommodating the sensory needs of autistic children is always part of the solution to social inclusion.

Social Stories™ were invented by Carol Gray in 1991. A social story is a story that explains the perspectives of a given situation and helps the autistic person to understand the social information they need. The story then suggests ways of reacting and interacting that gives the person a choice and confidence to deal with that situation. Social stories teach social skills and enable the person to understand the what, where, when, how and why of a situation, event or relationship.

This book will take you through the rationale for using social stories to explain social information to children with autism, when to use them and when another strategy might be best. It will explain how to write and edit them to personalise them for the child you work with and how to present them to the child and read it with them. Included is a CD-ROM of editable stories to explain common situations in a primary school that autistic children often find difficult; these are intended to be a bank of templates to start you off.

The best stories are those that are personal and 'owned' by the child and that change something in their understanding so that they feel more positive and confident with a situation they previously found confusing and difficult.

Chapter 1
Autism and social understanding

Autism is a different way of thinking.

In the last ten years or so, there have been more and more children diagnosed with Autism Spectrum Disorder (the term used by clinicians and the *Diagnostic and Statistical Manual of Mental Disorders* (2013) diagnostic criteria). More teachers have taught autistic children in the classes they have had, and training to support autistic pupils is becoming more widespread and is planned to be part of initial teacher training (ITT) in years to come. Many schools want to adapt so they can support their autistic pupils and see them thrive. In order to do so, they need to understand the world through the eyes of each autistic child.

Research shows that the autistic brain is 'wired' differently and that the way an autistic child experiences, perceives and thinks about the world is different from a neurotypical child. Their development and interactions may be very different from the other children in your class or at home, or they may be very good at imitating and masking the real difficulties they have in coping with the demands of the world around them. Autism is a spectrum condition, each person is different and has their own unique set of strengths, skills and weaknesses. They may do things differently and not be able to work out why people don't understand them or understand why what others do is so confusing.

Communication

In autistic children the spectrum of communication abilities and difficulties is vast. A child may be pre-verbal, have no speech and communicate through behaviour and actions. Conversely, a child may have an excellent vocabulary and be able to speak at length about topics and subjects they are interested in. An autistic child may use echolalia, which is when they echo words and phrases from their memory in order to try and find the right words to communicate. At other times echolalia is a verbal stimulation that the child enjoys. What most autistic children have difficulty with is understanding the communication of other people. They may often have difficulty communicating effectively in socially demanding situations. Reading non-verbal communication can be difficult too. Some children can be quite literal in their understanding of what is being communicated because they have missed the gestures, facial expressions, body language, tone, inference, context and implied meanings of what other people are saying. Some children take longer to process verbal language and so misunderstand or miss some of what is being communicated. They might then find it takes them so long to reply, respond or understand what is happening that the situation has moved on without them. Some autistic children can be confident speakers on the surface, but the constant effort needed to interact with others can be so exhausting that they are not able to function for some time afterwards.

> *It is often that others are poor communicators to the child with autism that causes them the difficulty.*

If we take the opportunity to communicate in a way that the child with autism can understand, and give them time to process it, we can then be more successful in our communication with each other.

Social interaction and understanding

Much of a child's day involves social demands, from interactions with parents and family when they get up in the morning, to interactions with peers walking into the school playground and with teachers going into class. Going out in the community, shopping or clubs after school means there are social demands from morning to bedtime. Autistic children need to put in a lot of effort to deal with all these demands.

For some children the demands themselves are difficult to interpret, too fast to process and overwhelming. They may already be trying to cope with sensory messages from the environment that take up a lot of their processing ability. Tuning into the right person, shifting attention between people and 'reading' the situation can be very difficult. Other autistic children may be focusing very hard to work out what is happening, what they should do and how they should react. For some, they become expert imitators and can seem to be managing well, but underneath they carry much anxiety about what to do, how to react and respond. They can easily become exhausted through the effort of trying to 'keep up' and constantly being worried about whether they are getting it right or not. Feedback from others may be very difficult for them to interpret, because many 'signals' are subtle, fleeting and can mean multiple things depending on the context. This will impact on their ability to understand other people's points of view and perspectives. They may interpret social cues and the context in a different way and so miss some common assumptions, such as knowing when someone is joking or that someone is sad because their rabbit died. The interesting thing is that many autistic children can communicate very well with other autistic children.

> *Children with autism do have empathy but can have difficulty recognising the reasons for someone's sadness or other emotion.*

Most autistic children want to be involved and interact with others. There may be times when they prefer their own company, but not many are isolated by choice. Some children display what is interpreted as inappropriate behaviour, for example, a child taking an object from another child to indicate that they would like to play with them is often misinterpreted as snatching, and the reactions of others would be to complain or tell the child off. If we see this instead as an attempt to communicate, then the interaction could be much more positive. Many children become withdrawn or isolated because their experience of interactions has been so negative. This increases their anxiety and can lead to mental ill-health.

The stories in this book can help to explain how social interactions can be developed and also help other people understand the perspective of the autistic child so that social interaction can be successful for all involved.

Sensory processing

An autistic child may find the sensory information from the world around them overwhelming. They have difficulty tuning into the information they need to understand to know what is going on, such as the teacher's voice. This can lead to great distress for some children, and they often try to avoid the sensory activities or sensations that are too much for them. A common example is that of noise.

> *A classroom or echoing school hall can sound like a jumbo jet engine in the brain of an autistic child.*

Lighting, temperature, movement, personal space, touch, smells and tastes can all contribute to sensory overload. These children need support to **calm** their sensory system in order to be able to function more capably in the classroom environment. Other children may have difficulty registering sensory information and so be unresponsive or need to seek out more information to **alert** their system.

A child's perception of an activity, environment or interaction can be largely dependent on their sensory experiences. Too much distress can mean they display negative responses, or that they meltdown or shutdown. Something like a computer crash happens in the brain and the child is unable to function. They **need to be safe**, they need staff and carers to **not overload them** with more sensory information, such as talking to try and calm them down, and they **need time to recover**. We should do all we can to help the child avoid sensory meltdowns and shutdowns.

> *Sensory regulation is used to become calm or alert enough to be able to interact and learn.*

When we look at using social stories to explain situations to autistic children, understanding their sensory perceptions and differences will help us understand what it is we need to explain and what accommodations will be important for them.

Rigid and repetitive behaviours

One of the diagnostic criteria for autism is rigid and repetitive behaviours. These can include intense interests, collections, in-depth knowledge of specific subjects and repetitive physical behaviours such as hand flapping, rocking or spinning objects. An autistic child may be able to hyper-focus on their specific interest and want to know ALL there is to know about it. Whilst this has many advantages, it can also be seen as unusual when the child is with non-autistic peers who are talking about a variety of topics and subjects and may not be interested in the same things. Physical activities such as flapping, spinning or fidgeting can be ways in which the child is regulating their sensory systems and be something that is essential to enable them to stay calm and engaged in everyday activities.

Autistic children's emotional systems may also need regulating. Some children find recognising and communicating their emotions difficult, whereas others may be hyper-emotional, feeling every nuance and reaction as intense emotion which can easily overwhelm them. Repetitive actions can help regulate these intense emotions.

Autistic children are also likely to need routine and support when things change. One reason can be that they can find it difficult to imagine what something will be like. This involves having to predict a scenario and then make plans about how they are going to manage it. Having this flexibility of thought can be difficult in many autistic children, but it is often something that they can develop.

The need to be in control may be strong in some children who find the world confusing and frightening because they cannot predict what might happen.

Some children have rigid rituals and routines they must go through, others may seek to control through organising people and events to try and make them more predictable.

Special and intense interests provide confidence, enjoyment and happiness for many autistic children. It is important to include and celebrate what they are good at and build their confidence in other areas through what they know and can excel at. It may be something that isn't directly related to what you are doing, but the most creative teachers will harness and work with special interests. We should not be trying to change a child's special interests or forbid them from engaging in them. When we are using stories to explain situations to an autistic child, we can involve and refer to their interests to make the story relevant. For example, a child who loved history was encouraged to learn about recycling by studying how rubbish was thrown into the street in medieval times.

Chapter 2
Why we use Social Stories™

The structure and format of writing a Social Story™ is effective and should always be followed to ensure that you are writing a story that will support and help rather than overload the child with information and instruction.

Gray (2015)

Stories take many forms, from fiction and memoirs to factual accounts. Some stories try to teach a moral lesson while others challenge our views and introduce the spectrum of human characteristics. The written word, especially in stories, has the capacity to help us learn many things about other people and gain understanding of things that may be beyond our experience. Being written down means it can be returned to time and time again.

A social story can give a child the social information, understanding and positive options for managing situations, experiences and events that they might be confused or anxious about.

Social interactions are part of everyday life and are very difficult to avoid, especially at school. An autistic child may struggle with the number and complexity of demands all at once, all whilst dealing with sensory issues, anxiety and possible processing delays.

How well an autistic child copes with a socially demanding situation depends on many factors, such as their verbal confidence, familiarity with the people they are interacting with, trust of the people they are interacting with, context,

Show attention

Understand not just what they say but what they mean

Read the social inference and unwritten rules

Understand expectation, thinking and feelings of the other person

Solve a problem

Predict other's intentions

Think of a suitable response

Understand and predict the consequences of their response

Create the language needed for the response and quickly

Wait for the appropriate time to respond

Demands of a social situation

time of the day, skills of the other participants, their past experiences having being positive or negative and the sensory conditions.

Autistic children may prefer to be on their own or do things their own way, or they may long to have strong and inclusive relationships. We are aiming to guide them through school life and into adult life by providing the skills to deal with the situations they need to interact with.

As we will see in *Stories that Explain*, the stories are designed to support good, clear and explicit communication. This may include visual pictures and symbols which explain and support the text or speech.

Carol Gray's Social Stories™ (2010 & 2105) are written with a specific goal and are a useful tool in supporting autistic children to understand social situations and prepare them for new experiences. They provide a structure, an explanation and a reassurance that the child can navigate the situation. They are permanent and provide clear and uncomplicated language that is literal and unambiguous. They encourage and praise the child and, most importantly, give them the social perspective that they are missing so that they can understand the 'bigger picture' of the situation. They are personal to that child.

Social stories can cover almost any subject. If written and presented well, they can help a child learn, grow, deal with stress and build their confidence. Many schools are advised to use social stories for their autistic pupils, and they are included as a strategy on Education, Health and Care Plans (EHCP). Educational psychologists, SEND advisors and speech and language therapists may recommend using social stories, but it may seem quite daunting for teachers and teaching assistants to actually write one for the child in their class.

Key points about social stories

- A social story is written for an **individual** and is a **visual and permanent piece** that **describes and explains a social situation**, issue, event or skill that the child is finding difficult to understand.
- The aim of a social story is to **provide the social information** that the child is missing or misunderstanding so that they can make informed and **supported choices** about **how** they are going to **respond** in a more appropriate way.
- Although many social stories are written to **deal with difficult situations**, Carol Gray states that at least half of all social stories should be **written to affirm and celebrate the child's achievements**.
- A social story gives the child an explanation about the **perspectives of others**; their beliefs, opinions, common social

conventions, likes and dislikes, and often explains **'why'** people do the things they do.

○ When thinking about **behaviour**, we are aiming for **better understanding** of the situation **from the child** that will lead to them making more **appropriate responses and choices** because they **understand** that it will lead to **better outcomes** for them and for others.

Social stories are not magic. They don't 'deal' with a situation or make it go away. They don't make someone behave the way you want them to. They are not a tool to tell a child off or reprimand them for their mistakes or challenging behaviours. Poor social story writing can damage the relationship and trust the child has in an adult and can be dangerous. Imagine if the child takes the story literally, if you use words like 'must' and 'must not', then they have no way to choose what might be best for them in a situation. Autistic children and adults are at risk of being taken advantage of and being manipulated or abused by others. Social stories are not a 'one off' event, they need to be revisited on a regular basis to allow the child to build up their understanding, and they need to be flexible enough to be adapted if circumstances change.

> *The aim of social stories is to frame and communicate choices and keep children safe in socially complex situations.*

Accurate and well-written social stories can illuminate the world for autistic children. They can give them knowledge, insights and options to manage all kinds of situations. They can build skills, confidence and learning in ways that are accessible to them, acknowledging their needs and giving them opportunity to contribute to the story. The best stories are those written with the children.

Chapter 3
Using *Stories* that Explain

"As we write Social Stories™, the successful exchange of meaning is not assumed – it is a goal that we work very, very hard to achieve. We must carefully choose words and format most likely to be the effective messengers of our information. In addition, our stories enter minds that are unique, in some ways unfamiliar to us, and often very young."

Carol Gray
Howley & Arnold (2005)

Stories that Explain offers you guidance on how social stories are written and provides a comprehensive editable bank of story templates that cover a wide range of themes and situations that can occur regularly in school or at home for a primary-aged child.

The templates are for teachers and parents of autistic children to use which promotes working together as a team to support the child. Each story template can be edited to match the situation you want to help with or teach the child about. The stories can also be used with children who are not autistic and in fact are a good tool to communicate social interactions with any child who struggles to understand a social situation.

Stories that Explain guidelines

The stories are written in short paragraphs of 1–2 sentences wherever possible. Using the guidelines set out by Carol Gray they are written in **first**

person language which helps the child have ownership of the story, except for common and negative behaviours which are written in **third person**. This is so that the child does not feel that the story is targeting them and telling them off. Third person narrative shows that these responses and behaviours are common to other people too – which is important social information. Autistic children can often worry about why they seem so different: *Stories that Explain* can help them understand their commonality.

Each story has a **title** that describes exactly what the story is about. It is positive and reassuring for the child.

Each story uses **descriptive sentences** to describe the event, situation or issue.

Perspective sentences are used to explain the social information that the child may be missing or needs help to understand.

Directive sentences are used to explain what choices the child has to react or interact in that situation.

Affirmative sentences are used all the way through the story to reassure and praise the child that this is a positive story, and the difficulties they or others have are okay.

There are other kinds of sentences in social stories. These are: **partial sentences** which create spaces for the child to add their ideas and responses to the story and **co-operative sentences** where there is space for the child to coach their peers and adults who help them about how they would like to be helped. For the purpose of this book these sentence types are used minimally in the story templates provided, but questions and suggestions for the child to add their own ideas should be encouraged when using a story.

As reminders to personalise the text, you will notice that many of the stories have options for you to choose from, such as *she/he*; *mum/dad/other*; *a book/sensory box/toy*. Together with the child you are writing the story for, edit these as appropriate for their situation.

One main illustration is provided with each story, but I would recommend that you personalise and add more illustrations that break up the text further and make it relevant for the child; you can also use photos and pictures personal to them or the situation.

Choosing a story template

The story templates are written to cover some of the many common events experienced by autistic children in school and at home. Each **title** expresses what the story is about, and this helps the child know what to expect from the story. It should be reassuring and helpful. Choosing the right story for the situation is important. Understanding the child's perspective is our starting point. Asking the following questions may help you choose the right story for the child and the situation.

Assessing why you need a story

First you need to assess the situation you are faced with and look at whether a story needs to be used or whether another strategy might be more useful. Rushing into using a story can be disastrous.

> *The first questions to ask are:*
> - Is the child missing some social information that is causing them to react/act in the way that isn't successful for them?
> - How is the child feeling about this situation?
> - What is the main source of their anxiety?
> - Ask the child to say what they think about the situation. Observe them and how they react when you talk about it or when they are involved in the situation.
> - Don't assume you know what the child is thinking. Ask questions, find out what makes them really anxious or what they might be misinterpreting, and be prepared that their perception of the situation can be entirely different to yours.
> - Are there sensory barriers for the child?
> - What do you want to teach, prepare for or change for the child?

I would strongly dissuade you from just printing out the story and giving it to the child as it is. Even if you think it explains the situation perfectly, time spent personalising and checking the story for accuracy in each situation is likely to be much more effective.

Understanding who the story is for

Firstly you need to consider the child's ability to read, their processing speed and how much information they can process at once. Sometimes the story will not be suitable for a non-reader, and in the next chapter there are tips on how to adapt a story for younger children or non-readers. This list can help you gather the information before you begin using stories and should be updated as the child grows.

> *The first questions to ask are:*

- o How does the child communicate with you?
- o How long does it take the child to process what has been communicated to them?
- o Can the child read?
- o Can the child easily understand what they read?
- o Could the child understand symbols or photos better?
- o How much information would the child be able to understand in one go?
- o What motivates/interests the child? Can this be used in a way that makes sense in the story?
- o What can you celebrate and praise about the child in this story?
- o Is the child missing some social information that is causing them to react/act in the way that isn't successful?

You can involve the child in personalising their story working with a trusted adult can help them feel that the story is theirs.

Illustrating the story

Illustrations are used in the story to break up the ideas in the text. They are also there to enhance the comprehension of the story for the child, to ground it in familiar places and with familiar people and to help them focus into the key information.

Illustrations can tell the story without the words, especially for a non-reader or younger children and for those who can only process small chunks of information at once. Choosing the pictures to go with the text is as important as the text itself. Choose illustrations that mean something to the child and suits their developmental level.

Drawn pictures, as used in the story templates in this book, or clipart from the internet can be used to further illustrate the stories. These have the advantage of being more general and only having the focus information in the picture. Some children like cartoon-like pictures that bring humour into the story or pictures that have their favourite TV character in.

I once wrote a social story about why keeping kit tidy in the changing room was a good idea and used a child's favourite football player as an example of

Drawn picture used to illustrate 'Practicing for the play/concert' story template

someone who knew how to keep his kit tidy (with photographs courtesy of the football club's website). The child immediately wanted to emulate his hero and became the child with the tidiest kit in the class!

Photographs are easy to take and are suitable for any age. The child can see exactly the place, people and events you are including in the story. They are accurate and concrete, but be careful to frame them carefully. Autistic children can sometimes find it difficult to focus on the details in the picture that you want to point out to them, so be aware of backgrounds and lighting, additional people and objects that might confuse them. You can also highlight or put a border around the most important information they need to attend to. Too much specific detail can mean a child interprets the situation literally and will only follow the suggestions in the story if the aspects in the photograph are present, such as only when they are wearing the same clothes or are in that exact place. Being able to generalise the information will need careful planning if a child is very literal.

Symbols are commonly used for visual timetables and other visual supports for autistic children. Using them in stories can be a familiar and helpful illustration that the child knows and understands. Sometimes symbols can be useful in illustrating sensitive issues like toileting or personal care. They are factual and unambiguous without being gratuitous.

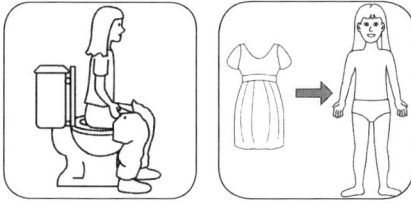

Personal care pictures. © dotolearn www.dotolearn.com

Once you are happy with the personalisation, layout and illustration of the story, you are ready to read it with the child.

Presenting the story

Remember the purpose of the story is to help, reassure and support the child in understanding a situation that has been, or will be difficult for them. If you are using the text as it is on the template and you are happy that the story will be meaningful for the child, then you can go ahead and read it with them.

You may want to laminate your story for longevity, but this is not usually necessary unless the child likes to tear paper. Print more than one copy so that you have a spare and can send a copy home for parents to read with their child at home. Involving parents in the process is the best way to enhance the learning for the child or it may be that you are a parent reading and using the stories from this book and sharing them with your child's teachers.

The story usually needs reading a few times to the child over the first weeks after introducing it and can be read by different but familiar trusted people. The frequency with which you read it with the child needs to be right for them. Some children love to keep their stories themselves and refer to them when they need to. Others get fed up with the story after a while (but this is often because they have moved on and have been able to deal with the issue confidently). You don't have to call it a social story. I often tell children that the story is just an explanation of what we have discussed and a record of how we are going to try to solve a problem or make a change. If it is a celebratory story, then it could be called a record of achievement.

If the child has a negative reaction to the story, becomes upset or refuses to read it, it is best to put it aside and review whether the content is suitable, if the tone used to read it was demanding or negative, or if the story just isn't explaining the right issue.

Story-sharing tips

o   *Think about where and when you will share the story with the child, and try to choose a calm and relaxed time and place with minimal distractions.*

o   *The child may want to read the story to themselves, or you can read it to them (particularly the first time).*

o   *It is important to read it slowly. Allow time for the child to process the language and for them to respond if they so wish.*

o   *Speak in a patient, calm and positive tone.*

o   *Once the story has been read, you can ask the child what they think about it or explain the activities you are going to do to support them.*

o   *Keep the story somewhere the child can access.*

Chapter 4
Supporting early skills

Shared attention, social imitation and symbolic play impairments in autistic children can often be an indicator of poor social understanding and interaction later on.

Toth et al (2006)

An autistic child may follow a different developmental trajectory than a neurotypical child. Their differences may mean that they miss some developmental milestones whilst their brains are working hard on other developmental areas. We often say that a child with autism can have a 'spiky' profile, especially when we are measuring them against typical developmental indicators such as the Early Years Foundation Stage Profile.

Social skills start early in a child's life, with babies being able to interact, respond and share attention with those around them. These early skills in autistic children may develop in a different way or be late to develop, and early language and communication skills may also be affected.

Frith (1989) and Cumine, Dunlop and Stevenson (2010) explain that young autistic children have weak 'central coherence' which is a difficulty with forming a 'whole picture' understanding of a situation. Children may be able to notice a lot of the details around them or focus their attention on something that particularly interests them; they may be fascinated by patterns or drawn to sensory objects or activities. However, being aware of the social world around them with the multitudes of movements, gestures, facial expressions, meanings, verbal instructions and sheer amount of choice, may seem to pass them by. The myth that autistic children are in their own world can stem from this. In reality they are working out what the world means to them in their own way. It may be that what catches their attention is sensory stimuli or details of objects or events that fascinate them.

Using stories to explain the world around them can help with this. Choosing the right words and focus can develop their awareness of 'the whole picture' and how it relates to their immediate and perceived experiences.

Stories can be used alongside other strategies to develop a bank of understanding, skills and learning from the early years onwards. However, there is no magical ideal moment or missed threshold of optimum learning. An autistic child will keep on learning all their lives. They may need support, such as *Stories to Explain*, all their lives. The support should grow as they grow and help them learn new things. I have used stories to explain many situations to teenagers and adults with autism.

Routines, change and new experiences

In the Early Years Foundation Stage (EYFS) and Key Stage 1 (KS1), children are experiencing a lot of things for the first time, and there are also many well-established routines in a school that they have to learn and follow. Children with autism often have a preference for routines and the familiar, therefore new experiences, change and things that don't happen as they usually do can bring confusion and distress. Stories to explain what will happen, why it is happening and what they can do to manage and cope with the change can be helpful. Firstly a child new to a school may need stories that explain what the regular routines are, why we do things that way, and how to manage themselves and interactions with others in that routine. Later, children with autism may need support to manage and prepare for change.

Story templates to support routines, change and new experiences

- Coming into school (Stories 1a–b) (see the template on page 27)
- Going home from school (Story 2)
- Good listening when we sit on the carpet (Story 3)
- All about lining up (Story 7)
- Eating my lunch in the hall (Story 9)
- Wet playtimes (Story 15)
- A visitor and a special assembly (Story 33)

Coming into school

My name is ....

I am in .... class.

Usually on Mondays, Tuesdays, Wednesdays, Thursdays and Fridays I go to school.

My .... *takes me in the car/walks with me/on the bus.*

When we get to my school it can be noisy, with lots of children playing and parents chatting. This is too noisy for me. This is okay.

My teacher knows it is too noisy and busy for me. My teacher and I have made a plan that my .... can take me into school *just before/at 10 minutes to 9.00 a.m. before* all the other children can come in.

Then my .... can say "Goodbye" and *she/he* will go. I can go into school with my teacher.

This is so that I can put my coat on my hook, unpack my bag and sit in my place before the other children all come in together. I can look at my visual timetable to see what we will be doing today. This is helpful.

My plan is that I can have *a book/my sensory box/a toy* until all the children are sitting down and my teacher says "It's time to start our school day".

Then I can change my visual timetable and be ready for the day at school.

I have come into school and I am brilliant.

Well done me!

1a

Understanding social interactions and relationships

It is common for autistic children to gravitate towards the adults in the classroom, particularly in the EYFS and KS1. Interactions with others and personal relationships may be harder for them to develop. Therefore, opportunities to develop good friendships and relationships with peers should be a priority. Some autistic children are social imitators and seem to be getting on well with their peers (especially girls with autism). They may seem to be in control but also become easily distressed when things don't go as they were expecting or disagreements happen. Repairing and sharing in relationships can be difficult for all young children, and young autistic children may not have developed the skills to do so in the same way their typically developing peers might. However, in these situations, stories to explain relationships can be effective with all children. A personal story can be a group story where the whole class or group learn together what is happening, why, and what they might do to manage the situation or relationship better. Although the autistic child may have some misunderstanding we want to correct, social interactions are always a two-way process and others learning about the perspective of the autistic child is just as important.

Story templates to support social interactions and relationships

- Good listening (Story 4)
- I can do good waiting (Story 5)
- Taking turns is a good way to work in our class (Story 6) (see the template on page 29)
- Joining in with others at playtime (Story 11)
- Winning and losing (Story 18)
- Working with a partner in my class (Story 19)
- When we fall out, we can make friends again (Story 36)
- Someone new has joined our class (Story 37)

Taking turns is a good way to work in our class

My name is ....

I am in .... class.

In my class there are lots of children. Sometimes my teacher wants to choose children to do something at the front of class.

This is great. All the children in the class like to help our teacher and be chosen by *her/him* to do one of these things.

Sometimes I am playing a game or doing an activity with other children when only one person can have a go at a time.

Sometimes someone is playing with a toy or on the touch screen tablet that I want to play with, and I have to wait for them to finish with it.

Taking turns is a good way to make sure that everyone can have a go.

My teacher knows that all the children want to be chosen. *She/he* knows that I want to be chosen. My teacher likes to be fair and give all the children a chance to answer a question, help *her/him* or to have a turn with a toy, touch screen tablet or activity.

This means that different children are chosen to be first and that my teacher makes a list of whose turn it is: first, second, third, fourth and so on.

Sometimes I can be first, sometimes it will not be me but someone else. This is okay.

I can try to remember it's okay when I am not chosen to be first. It is a great idea to look at the list and do good waiting until it is my turn.

All the children in my class are learning to take turns. I can be good at taking turns too.

Well done me!

6

Skills and independence

"Neurotypical people learn social skills through instruction, but also have an enormous capacity to learn by observing and interpreting the behaviour of others. NTs are able to do this because they are able to interpret the perspectives of others."

Patrick (2008)

An autistic child can start school knowing nothing about how school works. Neurotypical children 'absorb' social information and expectations through watching others, imitating and responding to verbal instructions. Autistic children may not be able to learn these skills in this way. Working out the important information and how to respond may be difficult for them. It also involves being able to spontaneously understand what is socially acceptable and what is not.

Therefore, in the EYFS and KS1 it can be effective to teach 'how to be at school' through stories that explain the kinds of concepts, routines and situations that tell the child **what**, **how** and **why**.

Learning new skills and gaining independence is an important part of growing up and learning. The independent skills children will need to be taught will be different and change over time. There are many autistic children who are very academically able but poor at doing tasks and daily living skills independently. In the EYFS and KS1, all children are learning new skills and developing independence. Many autistic children need more structured support to learn to do something for themselves.

It is important to ask why they are finding something difficult to learn. A child who can't seem to feed themself may have significant sensory issues around food. Similarly with toileting. Other issues may be due to problems with executive function – the brain's abilities to organise, plan, predict, monitor own behaviour and emotions, start and complete a task. A child with these difficulties may not be able to sequence a task in their mind and carry it out to completion. The child may be experiencing motor difficulties and learning difficulties that mean they find it more difficult to learn the skill and do it independently. Without support for their sensory, motor, executive function or learning needs, a child may struggle to gain independence.

Often it is not a story that is needed to explain to the child the perspective or social information. Check whether another strategy may be better. It may be that what they need are some sensory strategies or therapy, practical support, a visual schedule or a different way of teaching.

If the child is struggling to do a skill or task independently because they don't see the purpose, then a story to explain that may be effective. If a child doesn't understand what the benefits are to them or to others of the skill or task, then a story to explain that may also be effective. An example is a child not using the toilet because they think it involves losing part of their body. We can explain in a story that using the toilet is good because it gets rid of all the waste from the food we eat. Or for a child who doesn't understand why we are clearing toys away, a story can explain that tidying toys away makes the classroom clear so the next activity can happen.

Story templates to support skills and independence

- ○ Coming into school (Stories 1a–b)
- ○ Going home from school (Story 2)
- ○ I can do good waiting (Story 5)
- ○ Going to the toilet (Stories 8a–c)
- ○ Eating my lunch in the hall (Story 9) (see the template on page 32)
- ○ Choosing different activities (Story 10)

Eating my lunch in the hall

My name is ....

I am in .... class.

At school we have a break to eat some food in the middle of the day. All the children go into the hall where there are big tables and lunchtime supervisors to look after us.

Some children can find it hard to eat in the hall. It is a noisy place, with lots of children chatting and moving around. Every day there are different smells and food that other people are eating. This can make me feel upset and not want to eat in the hall. This is okay.

I want to sit with my friends and they want to sit with me. My teachers are going to save a table for us near the door and away from the hatch where the food is served.

My friends know I like to have a space next to me. This is okay. They will leave a space.

My friends and the lunchtime supervisors know I like to eat my food in the right order. This is okay.

My friends and the lunchtime supervisors know that sometimes I wear my headphones. This is okay.

When we have finished, my friends will be happy to help me put my rubbish in the bin and go out to the playground together. I like this.

If I am feeling upset or the smell is a really horrible one, I can choose to sit in the classroom with my friends and we will eat our lunch there. I can decide by visiting the hall just before lunch to see what food smells there are today.

I like going to eat my lunch with my friends. We will sit on the same table and eat our lunch together. Then we will go out to play.

This is great.

9

Teaching and learning

In England the first years of school are supported by the EYFS, Scotland has the 3–5 Curriculum and Wales the Foundation Phase Curriculum. Autistic children's development may follow an atypical pattern. Therefore it is important to chart the child's progress accurately and note their strengths and weaknesses. The areas covered by the curriculum are:

- ○ Communication and language development
- ○ Physical development
- ○ Personal, social and emotional development
- ○ Literacy development
- ○ Mathematics
- ○ Understanding the world
- ○ Expressive arts and design.

DfE (2017)

The curriculum guidance also states that teachers should support each child individually and give them meaningful and accessible activities to enable their development. This includes children with special educational needs and disabilities (SEND).

Stories that explain are not usually something that can be used to teach the curriculum, but they can support the understanding of the skill, knowledge or activity and make it meaningful to the child. When a child responds well to a story that is written for them, it can also be evidence that they have achieved one or more of the descriptors that staff need to record in the EYFS Profile.

Examples of stories that I have written for specific children to support teaching and learning include:

- ○ I know a lot about space and I can show my teacher what I know
- ○ We do different kinds of writing
- ○ Dinosaurs can help me learn about numbers
- ○ The computer is for doing work
- ○ Going outside can help us learn about science.

Story templates to support teaching and learning

- ○ Choosing different activities (Story 10)
- ○ Joining in with others at playtimes (Story 11)
- ○ Working with a partner in my class (Story 19) (see the template on page 34)
- ○ What I can do when I don't understand (Story 39)

Working with a partner in my class

My name is ....

I am in .... class.

I am really good at working in my classroom now. My teachers are very pleased.

Sometimes my teacher wants me to do a task with another child in my class. This is called working with a partner.

Working with a partner means that there are two people with ideas and they have to decide how to use both ideas in their work. It is a good idea to have some 'Working with a partner' rules.

My partner today is ....

Working with a partner rules

1. Take turns to speak. Do good listening when your partner is talking.

2. Write down what each person's ideas are.

3. Choose one idea to start with. Sometimes this is your idea, sometimes it will be your partner's idea. This is good partner work.

4. Make a plan of what you will do first, next and then. Write it down and follow the plan.

5. Take turns to do things, or decide which part you will do and which part your partner will do. Don't forget to share out the work equally!

6. Do the work.

7. Put it together.

8. Be proud of and pleased with your finished work and that you did great partner working.

19

Behaviour

Confusion can lead to frustration, misunderstanding and stress. This may display as anger or challenging behaviour, or it may be that the child withdraws into themselves. Autistic girls are likely to be more socially aware but just as confused about the social conventions and unwritten rules of interacting with others. They can mask their difficulties and often resort to imitating others to find a way to 'fit in'. This leads to great anxiety and a risk of mental health issues as they grow up; this is true for both autistic boys and girls. At times they can be aggressive and controlling, but all these strategies are their attempts to manage distressing and stressful situations and we should see them as so. Some autistic children are very compliant, terrified of getting into trouble and seemingly very shy. They too would benefit from support to understand social situations and build their confidence.

Behaviour is part of how we communicate and gives us clues to how the child is feeling, what they are interested in and what they find difficult.

Understanding what the child is communicating through their behaviour depends on us, the adults, to interpret that behaviour.

Stories that explain are not supposed to 'deal' with behaviours. (Unfortunately, I have read many so-called social stories that do just that.) They should explain to the child **why** something is happening and **what** they can do to manage that situation **when** it occurs. We want to affect behaviour and see positive outcomes but not insist that they should be doing something that doesn't make sense to them. If we dictate to the child **you must** and **you should**, then all they do is learn to respond robotically to a stimulus or threat – especially when there is a negative consequence prepared.

What we want is the child to:

- o understand what is happening
- o understand what the meaning and motives of others are
- o recognise what perspective information will help them understand why it is happening
- o be able to act upon this knowledge and interpret why there may be a better behaviour or action they could do in response
- o understand what they will get out of it.

All human beings are motivated by getting their needs met, or by rewards. The reward does not need to be a treat, it just needs to be positive to the person who is being asked to do something and change the response they previously had to a situation. This can be used to support a child when they have strong emotional responses such as anger and frustration. We can help children know when and how to ask for a break or help. We can support them in understanding their emotions and what their strategies and supports are to be able to self-regulate (that is, calm or alert themselves to a safe and calm inner state). Using stories to explain a situation that is scary, threatening, overwhelming, confusing or maybe just boring to a child with autism can help them develop more appropriate communication and reactions and know that the support they need (such as headphones in noisy places) will be there for them.

Story templates to support positive behaviour

- I can do good waiting (Story 5)
- All about lining up (Story 7)
- Choosing different activities (Story 10)
- What I can do when I feel upset (Story 12)
- My brain and my senses (Story 13) (see the template on page 37)
- What I can do when I feel angry (Story 20)
- Gentle touching (Story 21)
- Sometime things happen by accident (Story 30)
- What I can do when I feel scared (Story 40)

It has been my experience (and that of Howley and Arnold, 2005) that a story for children being supported in the early skills works well when supported by further visual schedules or pictures that help as reminders. It is worth considering how we can help a child generalise the learning so that they do not see the story as being applicable in only one setting or context.

My brain and my senses

My name is ....

I am in .... class.

My brain works hard.
It makes sense of all the noise, movement, sights, smells, tastes and things I feel all around me.

My brain works hard.
Sometimes there is too much going on in my brain. Too many sensory messages all at once are not good for my brain. This can make me feel *anxious/scared/cross/upset/ excited/too full of energy**.

My brain works hard.
Sometimes there is not enough in my brain. Not enough sensory messages make my brain fall asleep. This can make me feel *lazy/tired/bothered/distracted/upset**.

My brain works hard.
I can help it be calm, awake and ready to work. This is great.

My brain works hard.
I can do some activities when they are on my visual timetable or when there are too many or not enough messages in my brain.

My brain works hard.
When it is calm and awake, I am ready to listen and work. Hurray!

I like being calm. Awake is good too.
I can try to help myself by using these activities when I feel anxious or can't do my work. When my brain is too busy or falling asleep, I can help it work better.

My brain works hard. I can help it be the best brain I need.

Well done me!

* Add/delete as appropriate.

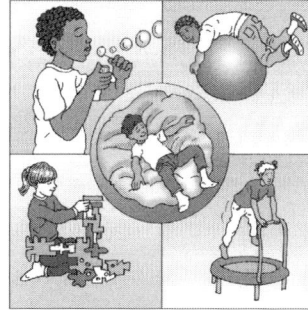

13

Using *Stories that Explain* with younger children

For children who cannot read, the pictures become the vehicle by which the story is carried. The text becomes the script for the adult and may need simplifying. The story may need more repetitive refrains or smaller chunks of information.

A story for a younger or non-reading child will need to use photographs or illustrations to show what is happening. It should be that the child can 'read' the story from the pictures with some key words to support each picture. Perspective becomes more difficult to communicate in this context, and you should choose carefully illustrations that communicate what other people might be thinking. (Remember that each sentence and photograph may need to be on a separate page.)

In this context, the text becomes simpler sentences that are a script for the adults who read the story to the child. This provides repetition and consistency which can be really helpful and reassuring for the child.

Case study

George in Year 1 didn't like lining up. When the teacher told the class it was time to line up, he would not respond. The teaching assistant would get hold of his hand and lead him to the line and then leave him as other children joined the line behind him. George would soon be pushing and shoving the other children, and that would lead to him nipping and hitting the child in front of him. Loud cries of complaint and injustice were heard from the child who had been hit and usually George would then be told off, taken out of the line and made to stay in class with the teaching assistant whilst the other children went off to the activity they were going to.

The teachers had noticed that George rushed to the front of the line when they lined up in the playground to come into school and was always the first in the class, but every time the class was to move around school his behaviour became distressed and aggressive towards his teachers. He was missing out on assemblies, computer time, the library and even lunchtimes had become a problem, with George fighting with other children on the way to the hall. They had temporarily made George eat his lunch in the classroom, taking up more of the TA's time.

Gathering information

Working out what perspective George had on this situation was the first priority. The teaching staff had tried all kinds of strategies, such as allowing him to go at the front of the line or the back of the line or walking with the TA, but nothing had worked.

Talking to George it became clear he was very anxious about lining up. He got very angry and said he hated school because they were always making him do things he didn't like. Further questioning revealed that what George was most anxious about **was not knowing where he was going** when the class was told to line up. To add to this, he was **hyper-sensitive to touch** and was scared the other children might bump into him and hurt him. He hardly ever heard what the teacher had said about where they were going due to the amount of noise when the class was tidying up or moving about into the line. When he was put into the line, his fear of the unknown place they were going and the anxiety about being touched was too much for him. He quickly worked out that if he hit the other children around him, it was likely that he would have to stay in class and not have to walk in the line or go to the unknown place, and this behaviour was working for him. We also found out that when he was on the playground, he rushed to get into school because he knew where he was going but still had the fear of someone touching him in the hustle and bustle of the lining up.

The story we wrote to explain the situation for George is 'All about lining up' (Story 7) (see the personalised version on page 41). The story explains what lining up is and why it helps the class move from one place to another safely. It also explains that George's teachers would let him know where they were going, how long he would be there and what he was going to do. With this we taught George that he could use a communication skill of his own. He could ask "Where are we going?", which meant that even if the teacher forgot, or if there was a substitute teacher, he could still find out where he was going. We also talked to the whole class about keeping a space between them and the next person and everyone practised this regularly. George also learned to say, "I need space please", instead of hitting a child.

The wording of this story is important. George is not told what he **must** do but what he **can** do. There are options for his reactions that are more behaviourally appropriate, and it **affirms** George by encouraging him to do what he can and, through understanding where he is going, that he can feel safe. We have also used the word 'usually' to cover if someone has to stay behind in class for any reason.

George listened to his story as it was read to him by his teacher. Photographs had been added so that the scene was familiar to him. The teacher walked him through the story with the class lining up together and talked to the other children about lining up and what George needed in terms of space and not to be touched. The story was read daily for about two weeks until George knew it and was lining up successfully. He loved being able to ask where they were going, and the other children would eagerly remind him to ask, particularly when there was a different member of staff asking them to line up. They wanted to know too.

All about lining up

My name is George and I'm in class 1.

There are lots of children in my class.

Sometimes we have to go out of the class and go somewhere else.

We might go to the hall, library, computer room or into assembly.

A good and safe way for all the children to move from one place to another is to follow each other in a line.

When the teacher says "Line up", I can go to the door and stand behind another person. This is good.

The other children in the class will usually do this too. This is good.

I might have someone standing in front of me and someone standing behind me. This is okay. If people touching me are too much, I can stand at the back of the line or hold the door.

I can ask "Where are we going?", and my teacher will tell me.

Where are we going?

When all the children are in the line, the teacher will take us to where we are going. This is great and everyone will keep safe.

It will be good if I stay behind the person in front of me and walk nicely without bumping into them, and they will try not to bump into me. This is good.

I can try to be good at lining up.

Well done me!

Chapter 5
Supporting later skills

"Most of the things we perceive in the real world are open to multiple interpretations. The world is intrinsically ambiguous. Stimuli do not have a fixed meaning but obtain their 'correct' meaning from the context."

Vermeulen (2013)

As children move into Key Stage 2 (KS2), the curriculum becomes more formal in most schools. The amount of work the teacher has to cover in a week is prescriptive and at a pace that can be challenging for some autistic children. Others may find the work well within their capabilities. As children develop through KS2 so do their friendships and relationships, and the challenges of understanding social situations become more complex. There is inference, sarcasm, teasing, jokes, knowing the boundaries within interactions, dealing with anxieties and new and unexpected events. Relationships between children become stronger and more fragile at the same time. Falling out, leaving out and establishing the 'pecking order' become part of the subtle daily interactions between children. It is often during these years that girls can be more identified as having autism, especially if they have masked their difficulties until now. Some will continue to mask, but others start to become more and more overwhelmed by trying to understand the social complexities that they show signs of anxiety and distress.

Supporting social understanding is important in KS2 so that the child can develop the confidence that will enable them to make the transition to secondary school and beyond. Being anxious about misinterpreting and misunderstanding any situation can be supported by a story that explains to them what is happening, why and what others might be thinking about it Context becomes very important too.

Vermeulen (2013) says that the details, and putting them together, are important, but that unless the child is able to read the context, then they will not be able to fully understand the event and what their actions and response should be. Understanding context can help keep a child safe as well as enable them to adapt, generalise and implement what they know. Not being able to do this seems to be, according to Vermeulen, one of the reasons why autistic children struggle to develop flexibility of thought.

An example is a child who has learned to play with friends in the playground at school but won't allow those friends to come to their home because that's not the place they play with their friends. Or a child who is allowed to go first in the line at school may expect to go first in the line when they are queueing up at the supermarket till.

Words have different meanings depending on the context. Providing the context information in a story can make all the difference to a child's understanding. For example, we might say, "Work at school is when we sit at a table to do an activity with the teacher or on our own. When we have done the activity, then usually, the work is finished." It usually isn't perceived as work when the child is doing a jigsaw at home or colouring in a sheet of pictures whilst waiting for food in a restaurant. As we develop early understanding, these supporting contexts can build up a greater understanding of how to take into account the wider situation.

In using stories that explain the world to an autistic child, we can write more effective stories by understanding the need for developing the understanding of context. This means that the words we use in our stories need to be chosen carefully, with a good understanding of the child's viewpoint of the situation. We mustn't assume we know what the child is thinking or experiencing, but try to gather all the information we need to check and make an 'informed guess' as to how they are perceiving the situation. We may need to explain words clearly in context and help them understand that in other situations the same or different rules apply.

> *When a child is likely to understand an explanation literally, then context is very important.*

We need to explain in the story the contexts in which something is appropriate and the contexts in which it is not. Greeting people is an example. Whereas greeting people at school or family at home is good, greeting strangers in the park or random passers-by can be more problematic. This provides us with a teaching situation to help keep the child safe.

Encouraging independence in routines, change and new experiences

We can encourage greater independence in KS2. Sometimes using a story to explain is not the strategy that is needed. For example, asking a child to get themselves organised for home time can be impossible for them when all the other children in the class are moving around, chairs are scraping on the floor, there is chatter, noise and verbal demands coming from all directions. In these scenarios management of the environment, a buddy and perhaps visual schedule supports can support the child to achieve a task independently, rather than needing a story.

However, if the child is unable to do a task or join in an activity independently because they are thinking about it in a way that is causing a barrier, or they need support to understand how they can do something successfully, be reassured or celebrate what they can do well, then a story to explain might be helpful. The story will be able to help the child process the information and understand the **why, how** and **what** to do. It explains and is communicated in a form they can more easily process.

We want a child to try new experiences and know how to cope with changes. These things can be very challenging for an autistic child if we don't support them or make the right adaptations. Changes can be unexpected or planned, small or big events, and can cause extreme amounts of anxiety. Stories that explain can make all the difference for an autistic child in whether they can even attempt something new. Knowing what will be the same and familiar is important to include too, as this is very reassuring for a child. There are many things autistic children have been able to do with a supporting story that their teachers or parents thought they never would be able to manage.

The story templates can be simplified for younger children, but for children in KS2, additional information such as reference to their abilities, successes and special interests can be added.

Story templates to support independence in routines, change and new situations

- Eating my lunch in the hall (Story 9)
- Wet playtimes (Story 15)
- Things sometimes change (Story 16)
- Being organised at home time (Story 24)
- A supply teacher is in my class today (Story 27)
- Practising for the play/concert (Story 31)
- Performing our class assembly for others (Story 32)
- A visitor and a special assembly (Story 33)
- Going on a school trip (Story 34)
- Going on a school holiday (Story 35)
- A school party (Story 38)
- When things change, I can be okay (Story 48) (see the template on page 46)
- Going for an appointment in school time (Story 50)
- Organising my bag for school (Story 56)

Understanding social interactions and relationships

As discussed in the beginning of this chapter, social relationships become more complex in KS2. Children are developing their communication and interaction skills and asserting their preferences amongst their peers. They are learning about give and take, compromise and repairing of relationships, often with the teacher's support. Autistic children may want to join in and interact with others and may want some time alone too. All children will have their own set of abilities and difficulties doing this. At this age the situations that arise can be more complex, the context more important and the responses we offer the child more flexible. They require choice and ownership of the response suggestions, for example, "I could ask my teacher where we are going or look at my visual timetable to see what is happening next."

As children reach upper KS2 they may be experiencing the early stages of puberty. Emotions and relationships can fluctuate widely and this is no less true for an autistic child. We should be acknowledging how a child is feeling, their sensory reactions and not dismissing these as unimportant. I remember reading a poor attempt at a story that said, 'It doesn't matter how angry you feel, you must not break the toys.' A much better way of phrasing this would

When things change, I can be okay

My name is ....

I am in .... class.

I live at home with ....

I like to know what my day is going to be like. It is important to me to have good routines and be told what I will be doing. My visual timetable helps me know this.

Keeping things the same makes me feel safe. This is good, and my parents and teachers understand this.

Sometimes things change. This can make me feel scared and upset. It takes my brain a long time to understand that something is different and work out what I need to do in the new situation. This is autism. This is okay.

It will be helpful if people at home and school tell me about a change before it happens. I can be helped by:

- being given time to think about the change – don't rush me
- seeing pictures
- putting the change on my visual timetable
- being able to visit the new place just to look beforehand
- being reminded of what will be the same, and that I can take my comforting toys/activities with me
- being shown how long it will last and what familiar things I can do afterwards
- or ....

It is part of life that things do change. It is okay that change makes me feel scared. I can try to remember that my parents and teachers will help me feel safe. They will make sure I know what I need to be able to cope with the new or unexpected thing.

I can try to remember that some changes are only for a short amount of time, and that some changes can be good. If it is a bad change, then I can try to remember that there are people who will help me. This is good.

When things change, I can be okay.   48

be, 'It is okay that some things make you feel angry. A good thing to do when you feel angry is _____. This can help you feel better.'

Acknowledging and validating emotions is a very important way of supporting a child's mental health and wellbeing.

Many situations are so bespoke that writing a story for each unique situation is often needed, however, there are still some common social interaction and relationship issues that regularly occur in many settings that the stories below can help to support.

Story templates to support social interactions and relationships

- ○ Winning and losing (Story 18) (see the template on page 48)
- ○ Working with a partner in my class (Story 19)
- ○ What I can do when I feel angry (Story 20)
- ○ Sometimes things happen by accident (Story 30)
- ○ When we fall out, we can make friends again (Story 36)
- ○ Someone new has joined our class (Story 37)
- ○ What I can do when I feel scared (Story 40)
- ○ Fighting on the TV and in video games is not real (Story 47)

Teaching and learning

In KS2 children are usually used to the teaching and learning activities that they are expected to do each day and will have developed a preference for some subjects over others and be more aware of their own abilities and learning difficulties if there are areas of the curriculum that they struggle with. The child's profile may have evened out or still be 'spiky' with abilities and difficulties in different areas. Often the child is a more able reader but when presenting a story to them, we need to remember that their ability to understand and process what they read may not be as good as their reading speed. Therefore, splitting the text of a story into chunks and providing illustrations that support the text is still important but can be made more age-appropriate through the text size and type of illustrations used.

Supporting the understanding of why they are learning things, independence in doing work tasks and being organised is important at this stage. An example is when one child didn't understand why he had to show his working out in maths. A story to help him understand the reasons was shared with

Winning and losing

It's always great to win a race or a game. It makes us feel good!

Sometimes I win. That's good! Sometimes someone else wins. That's good for them too.

Sometimes my team wins and we are really pleased. Sometimes another team wins and they are really pleased.

We can't always win, that would not be fair. Everyone should get a chance at winning.

When we lose, sometimes it can make us feel disappointed and angry. If someone is angry it can spoil everyone's fun.

We can all try to remember to be a good player and say "Congratulations", or "Well done", to the winners. This makes everyone feel good.

And when I win, they will say "Well done" to me too.

I am a good game player!

Well done me!

18

him. He would often check the story before he started a maths lesson where working out was required, and the teacher followed this up with a celebration of his ability to show his working out. The advantage for this child was that establishing this ability and understanding in KS2 set him up to be able to cope with the showing of working out that he would encounter at secondary school.

Story templates to support teaching and learning

- Being organised (Story 17)
- Working with a partner in my class (Story 19)
- Different kinds of writing (Story 23)
- I can do a test (Story 25)
- Showing my working out in maths (Story 26) (see the template on page 50)
- What I can do when I don't understand (Story 39)
- Doing school work at home (Story 46)
- Reading my reading book at home (Story 53)

Behaviour

"Although it is tempting, we cannot make assumptions about how someone is feeling based solely upon our perceptions of how we think we would feel if we were in their context or situation and then believe those assumptions to be true."

O'Brien (2015)

By looking more closely at how a child is behaving, we can learn from them what is driving that behaviour and work with them to find a more appropriate way of dealing with the issue. It may be that it is others who need to change their behaviour, or that it is the environment that needs to change. For example, a child who refuses to go into the hall for assembly may need to understand what is happening, what the point of assembly is and what they might get out of it. Conversely, they may need to have ear defenders, permission to leave if it is too much and a seat near the exit.

Blaming, punishing or enforcing sanctions should play no part in a story. A story should be about explanation, reassurance, affirmation and guidance.

49

Showing my working out in maths

My name is ....

I am in .... class.

I am good at maths. It is one of my favourite subjects. I know the answers quickly and can do the work really well. This is great.

My teacher might ask me to show my working out. I'm not keen on this because I know the answer, so it makes me feel annoyed when I am asked to show my working out.

It is my teacher's job to teach me how numbers and mathematics work. Usually mathematics is a sequence of steps to work out an answer to a problem. We show the problem in numbers, signs and sometimes letters.

Maths usually has right and wrong answers. If my answer is right, my teacher needs to check the sequences of solving the problem by looking at my working out. My teacher can tell that I am understanding all the maths at every stage. This is good.

When I get the answer wrong, my teacher can check my working out at each part of the sequence and check where the mistake was made. This is so that my teacher can teach me anything I haven't understood properly. This is my teacher's job. This is good.

Showing my working out teaches me to check my work carefully to make sure I haven't missed anything out. This can be really important!

This rocket crash shows the importance of showing the working out and checking your work!

On July 22 1962, at 9.20 p.m., the Mariner 1 spacecraft was ready for lift off. But less than five minutes into flight, Mariner 1 exploded. The reason: one small mathematical mistake.

26

Photograph of *Atlas Agena with Mariner 1* on Worksheet 26 from NASA

Challenging behaviour is mainly a challenge to the teaching staff who are trying to prevent and stop the behaviour from disrupting or hurting the child or those around the child. When preparing a story about behaviour that does challenge others, the time spent finding out why and what the child's perspective of the situation will be the key to getting the story right. Making our own assumptions often leads to a story being ineffective. We need to ask the child and help them work out what their perception of the situation is.

Case study

A child had a 'cross face' and was often kicking and doing 'karate' punches on other children. They would respond with similar behaviour to 'fight back' or complain to the teacher. This happened many times each day, and each time the child was receiving sanctions for his behaviour. When the child was asked about his behaviour to try to understand his perspective, we found out that he thought that it was just a normal way to interact with people because that's what he saw on his video games and TV cartoons each day. He couldn't tell the difference between the acting and animation on screen and the reality of those actions hurting others. We wrote a story titled 'Fighting on the TV and in video games is not real' which helped him understand the concept and supported this with a programme planned by the teacher of 'ways to play with my friends' which supported all the children to play more appropriately.

Story templates to support positive behaviour

- All about lining up (Story 7)
- Having a great playtime (a class story) (Story 14)
- Winning and losing (Story 18)
- What I can do when I feel angry (Story 20)
- Sometimes things happen by accident (Story 30)
- Fighting on the TV and in video games is not real (Story 47) (see the template on page 52)

Fighting on the TV and in video games is not real

My name is ....

I am in .... class.

TV and video game fighting is not real. On TV the people are acting, this means they are pretending. When they fight, it doesn't really hurt anybody.

TV cartoon and video game fighting is not real. The people are animations or drawings. They are not real and can't be hurt.

Fighting other children is real. People feel hurt and sore if someone kicks, pushes or punches them.

It is good to touch people gently, keep a space between you and try not to bump into them.

This is being real and respectful to others. They should try to be real and respectful to me too.

This is good.

47

Transition and new experiences at school

Moving classes at the beginning of each year can cause a lot of anxiety in autistic children and their parents. A new room, new teacher, new routines and different ways of working can be a lot to imagine. A story can be written to support this transition and prepare the child for the new experiences. However, what we can do first is remind them of **what will be the same**. In most new experiences there are many familiar aspects that we can remind the child of. This can help them feel more confident and able to manage the transition. The same can be done for a school trip and a residential visit.

When they are ready to leave the school to move on to secondary or another school, then a story can be written to celebrate what they do know, what they can do and include pictures to show what all the new things will be like (teachers, rooms, uniform, etc.). The story can explain what the child can do when they find themselves unsure of something and remind them of the support and help that is available. The transition should be supported by extra visits and the opportunity for the child to explain what they are worried about.

Case study

Alisha is autistic and finds new experiences so stressful that she often refuses to go into assembly and has never been on a school trip. Alisha's parents didn't want her to go on the school residential trip in Year 5 as they thought that the change and lack of routine would be too much for her. Her teacher thought that Alisha should go on the trip because she had made such good progress academically, she was much more independent in class and had two good friends that she was with most of the time at school. Both her friends were going and Alisha was starting to feel anxious but also kept saying she was sad and would miss her friends when they went on the trip.

Gathering information

Alisha thought her friends were going away forever and kept hugging them and telling them they mustn't leave her. She thought she wasn't allowed to go on the trip as she had overheard her parent's concerns. She said she thought she would like to go but was scared of trying so many new things and being away from home. Once we started to look at the photos of a previous trip, she became keen to go. The most motivating factor was that she could be with her best friends and share a room with them. She had never had a sleepover and thought this would be a good practice.

The story explained to Alisha just what was going to happen and that this trip was only for a certain amount of days and then everyone would come back to their own homes and usual routines. She was given time to explore the place they were going online and with her friends she put together a scrap book about it, the activities and one of the dormitories where it was agreed they could all sleep together.

The story explained to Alisha the purpose of a school holiday and acknowledged the fact that some children feel nervous and unsure about going. The tone is reassuring and informative and outlines the support that will be in place for her beforehand and whilst on the holiday. As with all stories, this one was illustrated with pictures between the paragraphs. In this case, photos of the previous year's visit to the activity centre were used.

This preparation and story that explained it all (see pages 55–56) enabled Alisha to go on the trip and have a successful time.

When they returned, Alisha's parents were thrilled that she had achieved such a huge step in her life and this gave them more confidence that she would be able to manage a move to secondary school eventually. She also had her first sleepover at her house with her friends.

Story templates to support transition and new experiences at school

- Moving to a new class in September (Story 22)
- Going on a school trip (Story 34)
- Going on a school holiday (Story 35) (see the personalised story on pages 55–56)

Going on a school holiday

My name is Alisha. I am in class 5.

Sometimes my school wants to take children on a holiday. This is when the teachers and teaching assistants travel to a place with the children and stay for 3 days.

This means that the teachers and children will have beds to sleep in at the holiday place. After 3 days and 2 nights, we will come home and go back to our usual routine of sleeping at home and being at school some days. This is good.

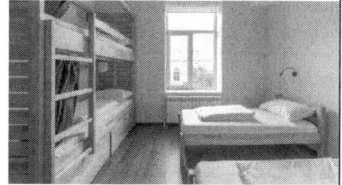

Schools organise holidays to help children learn things and try things that they usually can't do at school. School holidays can be fun with friends and teachers. Seema and Debbie are going to come too. I can stay in the same bedroom as Seema and Debbie. This is great.

The school holiday is at Beech Wood Outdoor Centre. The holiday will be from Tuesday until Thursday in the first week of March. Then we will come home.

In the day time there will be activities that all the children can try. They will be things we have done before and things that are new. There will be a timetable and information so that we can know what will happen and what to do. No one will be made to do anything they don't want to. But the teachers will try to make it work for everyone to have a try.

Some children feel very nervous about going on a school holiday because it is new and they don't know what it will be like. They might feel scared because they don't know what sleeping in a place that isn't their own room will be like. This is okay.

My parents and teachers will help me by showing me all the information I need and making sure that I know who will help me if I feel scared. My key person will be Mrs Smith.

I can look at Beech Wood on the internet with Seema and Debbie and make a book/collage of pictures and words that tell us all about it. I will be able to go and visit it on a quiet day before we go (my parents will do this with me).

When we go on the holiday, I can have my own visual timetable. My teachers can put this on a keyring so I can have it with me all the time.

morning	breakfast	canoeing	lunch
afternoon	climbing	free time	tea
evening	fire	shower	bed

Before we go, me, my parents and my teachers will make a plan that will support me when I am on the holiday.

Going on a school holiday is scary at first. This is okay. Lots of other children will feel a bit scared too. Even Seema and Debbie feel nervous. They are really happy that I am going too. Making plans, doing research and knowing the timetable can help me feel more in control. Maybe I can enjoy the school holiday and be proud of trying new things.

That would be brilliant.

Chapter 6
Personal awareness and problem solving

Autistic children may want to understand more about their autism and about their sensory processing differences. They may ask questions such as, "Why am I different?" and feel anxious about why things may be hard for them. They can learn from other people who are autistic, about autistic role models and to celebrate their personality. It takes time to come to appreciate their autism and a story that explains can help work towards this. This is an issue that is likely to need support throughout their life and the stories in *Stories that Explain* can build up a positive self-image and their self-confidence. Writing stories that explain the ways people communicate through body language, for example, or the way we touch others, can explain the way people generally interpret interactions. Understanding what to do when they feel emotions can also be helpful for personal awareness. You can write stories that explain the things they do well, what they have accomplished and that it is just okay to be themselves. Many children with autism cannot cope with compliments or praise, for example a story that explains what praise is, and how it can help them learn, can support this. These kinds of stories should make up more than half of all the stories you use. Praise stories should be bespoke and written for specific situations which is why there are not as many in this book as I would usually use in practice.

Story templates to support positive personal awareness

- What I can do when I feel upset (Story 12)
- My brain and my senses (Story 13)
- What I can do when I feel angry (Story 20)
- Gentle touching (Story 21) (see the template on page 59)
- I am autistic (Story 28)
- My friend is autistic (Story 29)
- What I can do when I don't understand (Story 39)
- What I can do when I feel scared (Story 40)
- Taking care of my body (Story 42)
- Sleep is good for my body and brain (Story 54)

Problem-solving skills

> *"Problem: A matter or situation regarded as unwelcome or harmful and needing to be dealt with and overcome."*
>
> **Oxford English Dictionary**

There will be times when you may want to use a story to solve a problem that the autistic child is having or creating. A problem here is defined as a situation that has occurred and the actions or outcomes are unwelcome or causing harm to the child or to others. This includes disruption to learning and the smooth running of the classroom. It includes situations where the child is distressed and cannot access learning for themselves and situations where others are causing a problem for the child.

Firstly **we must never see the child as the problem.** Autistic children are having to cope with many more challenges than neurotypical children and many of the difficulties they seem to create, such as disrupting learning and hurting others, will have roots in the child's attempts to cope with overwhelming challenges. By looking at a 'problem' objectively and thoroughly we can work out the root of it and work out what changes to make, explain the perspectives and affirm the child so that the things that will make the situation better can be implemented.

We can examine **our environment**: is it too sensory-stimulating? **Our communication**: are we talking too much and not giving the child chance to process what we are telling them? Do **teaching methods** make sense to the

Gentle touching

My name is ....

I am in .... class.

When I come to school in the morning, I go into the playground.

There are other children there too, and some of them are my friends.

I like my friends. I like to touch their things and hug them when I see them.

Some people like to be touched and hugged and other people find it really uncomfortable. This is okay. Everyone is different.

People can touch others gently or can squeeze them hard.

Some touching can hurt other people or they don't like it.

It is best to ask people if it is okay to touch their things or hug them.
If my friends say "Yes", then I can give them a quick hug and we can smile at each other.

If anyone says "No", I must not touch them. I can smile and say "Hello" instead. This is good.

People should ask me too. I can say "Yes" or "No", and they need to listen to me.

I am a friendly person.

This is great.

21

child? Is it the **best way** for them to learn? What about **the relationships within the classroom**: are other children teasing or picking on the child? By talking to the child and taking some time to observe them in the situation, we can hopefully find out what their perception of the situation is and use that as our basis for using a story that explains the situation.

Helping all children understand that life does throw up problems for each of us and fostering a positive attitude towards problem solving can help them feel less anxious, work it out and come up with solutions. This skill, taught and developed throughout the primary school, will help all children build resilience and confidence throughout their lives. Autistic children, however, may need much more support to develop this skill. Visual maps (Fig. 1 – editable version available on the CD-ROM) can be helpful. These can then lead to a story being written that is just right for the situation and that the child has made a major contribution to.

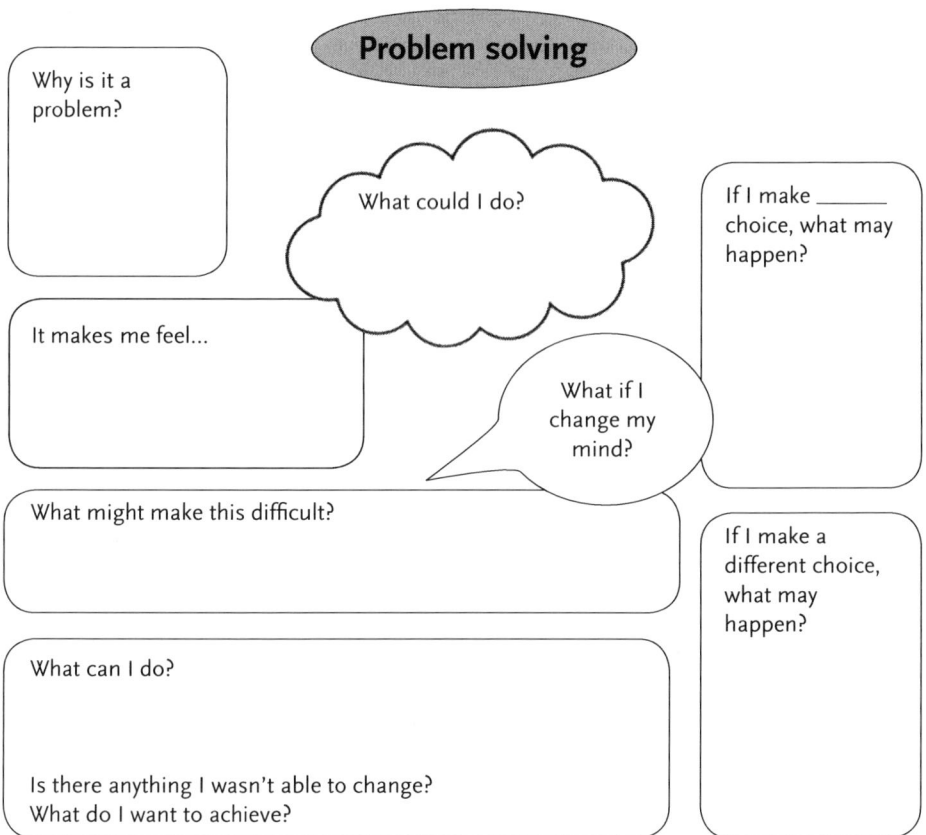

Problem solving

Why is it a problem?

What could I do?

If I make _____ choice, what may happen?

It makes me feel...

What if I change my mind?

What might make this difficult?

If I make a different choice, what may happen?

What can I do?

Is there anything I wasn't able to change?
What do I want to achieve?

Figure 1. Problem-solving visual map.

Story templates to support problem solving

○ Things sometimes change (Story 16)
○ Working with a partner in my class (Story 19)
○ Sometimes things happen by accident (Story 30)
○ When we fall out, we can make friends again (Story 36) (see the template on page 63)
○ When things change, I can be okay (Story 48)

Case study

Chloe is autistic and is a chatty, friendly girl in Year 3. She loves playing imaginative games with her friends at playtimes and writes wonderful stories often based on the imaginative stories she and her friends have been acting out at playtimes. She is academically able and loves doing jobs for the teacher. Chloe was having huge meltdowns at home after school, and her mum was worried that she was being bullied by her friends as she often cried and complained they were hurting her. The teaching staff noticed that Chloe was quite controlling and wanted her friends to play games as she directed. Her friends had gone along with this for some time but seemed to now want their ideas to be part of the story. Chloe and the other girls would hit out at each other when they didn't get their own way, and the supervisors at lunchtime were having to deal with many arguments and fallings out amongst the girls. Some playtimes Chloe was seen sitting on the bench on her own.

Gathering information

We spoke to Chloe to understand her perspective. Chloe was sure her friends hated her and because they had fallen out they never wanted her to be part of the group again. She was certain that friends never fell out and that she had destroyed any chance of having friends again ever in her life. She was feeling very lonely and angry with herself, rather than her friends. One particular argument had 'ended' the friendships, and Chloe was very upset about the fact that her friends had said they didn't want to play her games any more.

We brought all the girls together and used a problem-solving visual map to discuss what had happened. The solutions were made by the girls themselves, and we were careful to word it without blame or cause. The aim of the story was to enable Chloe and her friends to understand that they could work out a problem and that there were ways of making friends again.

We wrote in **first person for the introduction**, the description of the situation and affirming Chloe. We wrote in **third person to identify the problem** (people not wanting to do the same things and falling out about it) and for the **perspective sentences** (why people might shout and say unkind things). In this story we wrote 'we' for the **directive sentences**, as in **'what we'** could try to do about it, to reflect that this wasn't just about Chloe. The problem was something that the whole group was involved in, and the whole group had worked through together in their discussion. The ideas about what to do were their ideas. The illustrations this time consisted of the children's own drawings of playing together and celebrating their friendship.

Having this story written, illustrated and printed made it permanently available. Sometimes Chloe would get it out and read it herself, sometimes the group would be seen reading it together. They used it as a reminder of what to do if they disagreed, someone was upset or they just wanted to celebrate what great friends they were.

When we fall out, we can make friends again

My name is ....

I am in .... class.

I am a friendly person. I like to play with my friends and organise our games.
My friends are ....

Sometimes people want to do different things. This is okay. It is okay for me to say "No" when I don't want to do something. It's okay for my friends to say "No" when they don't want to do something.

Sometimes people like different things. They might not like the things I like. I might not like the things they like. This is okay. It can make people feel sad when people don't want to do the things they want them to.

Sometimes people shout and argue because they feel sad or annoyed. I might do that sometimes. My friends might do that sometimes. If people say bad things to others it makes them feel sad.

When people feel sad about falling out with someone they might say they are never going to talk to them again because they don't know how to sort it out. The other person might be feeling the same.

When people fall out it can be hard to try to make friends again. But people making friends again can be good. There are some things we all could try:

- Ask a teacher to help us.
- Tell the person the thing they said that was unkind.
- Explain how it made you feel and why something was hard for you.
- Apologise and understand that we may have said unkind things to each other.
- Agree that we will start again.
- Agree that it is 'sorted'.
- Decide on a different game or activity that we both like.
- Try the activity together.

36

Chapter 7
Using Social Stories™ at home

Stories that explain can be used in any environment, situation or setting. Parents and carers can find them useful at home, but rarely are parents given the training to be able to write them. Therefore, Carol Gray's book (2010) that can guide people in writing social stories and a book like this, with story templates, can be very useful.

In this book I have included some stories that have been used to bridge the gap between home and school situations such as doing homework, going to an appointment in school time and parent-teacher meetings. For example, a child who seems to be doing fine all day at school but then has a meltdown or shutdown as soon as they get home from school is often seen as not the school's problem. However, in most circumstances, the child is having a meltdown at home because they have a difficulty at school. This could be that they are so exhausted and overwhelmed by trying to keep it together through the school day that home is the safe place where they can let all that emotion, frustration and anxiety out. They may have nothing left in their energy stores to be able to function at home.

Home–school liaison

Situations that happen when home and school collide, such as parent-teacher meetings and being ill on a school day, can be supported by a story that explains what is going to happen and why. The autistic child may need some support to know how to manage and cope with the unexpected or different situation that may take them out of their usual comfortable routine. Choosing the story together with parents can be a great way to work cooperatively. They can provide additional information and suggestions that will work for their child. Having a copy of the story at school and at home can provide the child with security and predictability. They can learn to generalise and apply what they learn to the different settings which can help them understand adjustments that may need to be made in different contexts, such as understanding that there may be different ways of doing things at home and at school but both are okay and are different because of the context. For example, going to the toilet at home will be different from at school where there may be others going to the toilet at the same time.

Working with home to share the stories that explain situations that cross over both settings can strengthen the relationship between school and home and allow the school staff to understand the family's perspective. Communication of the child's celebration stories and strategies that are used to support the child, such as sensory activities, can be adapted for both settings if appropriate. Parents are generally pleased to work with schools, and hearing positive things about their child can build up their confidence in communicating and working with the school more too.

Story templates to support home–school liaison

- ○ Staying safe in the car (Story 43) (see the template on page 66)
- ○ Having a rest when I get home from school (Story 44)
- ○ Helping at home (Story 45)
- ○ Being ill on a school day (Story 51)
- ○ Wearing a school uniform (Story 52)
- ○ My *mum/dad* need to wash my PE kit (Story 55)
- ○ My parents are going to meet my teacher (Story 57)
- ○ The annual review (Story 58)

Parents using *Stories that Explain*

For those parents reading this book that want to use social stories, the advice in the earlier chapters is as relevant to home and community settings as it is to school, particularly the chapter explaining how to use the stories and adapt them to the individual child. Illustrations are important at home, and photos are often used by parents as modern technology makes this easier. If your

Staying safe in the car

My name is ....

I am in .... class.

When I am going somewhere, sometimes
I have to travel in the car.

My *mum/dad* usually drives the car because they have learned how to do it safely.
I have to sit in one of the passenger seats.

When I get into the car, I can sit in my seat and fasten the seatbelt around me.

Seatbelts were invented to keep everyone in the car safe. It is the *law/rule of the country* that everyone has to wear a seatbelt when they are travelling in a car.
This will keep my body safe. It is good to wear a seatbelt.

My *mum/dad* will tell me where we are going and how long it might take to get there.

I will have to sit in my seat with my seatbelt on until we get to where we are going and
my *mum/dad* says ".. you can get out now."

It is good to be safe in the car. I will try to be quiet while my *mum/dad* is driving.
I can *play on my touch screen tablet/listen to music/have my fidget toys/other* while
we travel to where we are going. Then they can concentrate on driving and we can
travel safely to where we are going.

Mum or dad will be pleased with me if I try to stay quiet and keep my seatbelt on.

Well done me. Brilliant!

43

child is able and willing, they can enjoy making the stories with you and then feel that they 'own' the story.

It may be that your child sees a social story as a 'school thing' and may not like to have them at home. My advice in this case is to call them something else. Make a scrapbook or presentation on the computer or use a social story app (Book Creator App is one I have used). The key is to use the same structure and types of sentences, remembering that the purpose of the story is to **explain** some social information the child cannot understand and to **celebrate** and **affirm** who they are. If written correctly, positive stories can describe a situation without mentioning the negative behaviours or impact on others. They can explain the positive consequences, meaning and reasons why the child can do something differently, try something new or feel proud of who they are.

Case study

When a family member is diagnosed with a life-changing illness or faces death, it can be a confusing and frightening situation for autistic children. Ben was in Year 4 when his dad was diagnosed with aggressive cancer. His parents had kept it from him until his dad was hospitalised. Ben's mum asked for help in explaining to Ben what was happening. She told us his dad was in hospital and unlikely to come home. They didn't expect him to live beyond another week. She was anxious about explaining this to Ben who now realised his dad was ill but was not aware of how serious it was. Ben was autistic and found it difficult to understand emotions. When other people were sad he laughed and when they were happy he didn't respond to their smiling and excitement. He would avoid people who were showing emotions he didn't understand although he loved to hug and cuddle his parents. He could sense other people's emotions and had empathy, but he didn't know how to respond and so withdrew.

Gathering information

Ben knew something was wrong in his family and had for some time. He thought his dad might be leaving and his parents getting divorced. He seemed relieved to know his dad was ill instead. However, he had never experienced anyone dying, and this was a concept his mum wanted to explain very simply. His mum said he would probably start to notice all the references to people dying, such as on the news or in the paper, and would want to talk about this.

Ben was often distressed when people cried or if he was in crowded rooms, and so this needed to be taken into account when we explained about the extra visitors. He needed routine and to know what would be the same whenever he faced a new situation, and he wanted to know that he could still go and do his favourite activities that helped him feel calm.

We wrote three stories to explain the situation to Ben. The purpose was to explain what was happening and that other people and he himself might feel very sad. In accordance with the family's beliefs, we explained that his dad was going to heaven, which was a good place, and that this meant he wouldn't be with the family any more. We explained what was going to be the same and how Ben could manage himself when he saw other people being sad.

The school and Ben's mum also planned some play therapy for him for after the funeral so that he could receive some bereavement counselling from someone who understood autism. The story shared with Ben was 'I can talk about someone who has died' (see the personalised version on pages 69–70).

The three stories were written to help Ben have time to process the death of his dad in his own way and time. We explained that other people may cry and look sad and that he didn't need to feel the same as everyone else. His mum found reading the stories with him helped them deal with the death together and led to them creating a memory book of photos and reminders of their time with his dad. He brought it into school and shared it with his classmates. Since writing these stories I have shared them numerous times with teachers and parents needing something similar. Dealing with sad events in the child's life is important. No one should assume that because a child doesn't react or show their feelings, they are not deeply affected by these events.

I can talk about someone who has died.

My name is Ben.

My dad is very poorly. He is staying in hospital so the doctors and nurses can look after him.

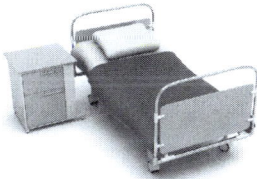

The doctors and nurses cannot make dad better. One day soon, dad will die and go to heaven. This means we will not see him anymore. It is good for dad because he will not be sick any more and is going to a good place. I will miss him. This is normal. My mum, my grandad and grandma and all their friends will miss him too.

People might feel sad because they will not see my dad anymore. They might cry. This is okay.

It is okay if I feel confused, sad or angry. It is okay if I cry or if I don't.

I could write or draw here what I am feeling.

😧 😞 😐 😊 😃

It will be good to remember and talk about my dad if I want to. I could bring things into school that remind me of him and tell my teachers and friends about them.

The people who will help me are:

At home _____

At school _____

Most people feel sad for a while and then start to feel better. Talking about and remembering the person can help. Some people feel fine about it and that's okay too. If I feel very sad it will help if I tell my mum or my teachers and they will try to work it out with me.

I can talk about my dad or other people who have died if I want to.
It is okay.

Conclusion

Using stories to explain situations, events and social activities to an autistic child can be very successful. They are creative, positive and helpful. However, if you have learned anything from this book, it should be that before you use a story for any situation, you should stop and ask yourself ,"Do I really need a story to explain this situation?"

Autistic children rely on their parents, carers and teachers to support them through their childhood years, through their education and through the myriad of socially demanding situations they are faced with. Our own understanding of their perspective can make us the people they can trust and rely on to help them navigate life's challenges. We can enable them to develop confidence, mutual friendships, enjoy what they like and learn new things that they may have never have learned without our help. We can help them learn about themselves and know how to be assertive when others make life difficult for them.

Social stories, as Carol Gray intended them to be, are only one of the approaches we might choose to use. In my experience, they help some autistic children in amazing ways.

> It can be like a 'lightbulb' moment when they suddenly or gradually understand something for the first time, and that gives them the confidence to approach the situation in a new and more confident way.

All of life's events can be celebrated, explained and navigated through using stories to explain. When you become more confident, you can write them about wider issues ranging from fears to world events. I have written social stories explaining why we have two minutes' silence on Remembrance Day. I have written stories that explain political events and disagreements amongst friends. I have discussed issues such as bullying, fairness and privacy with autistic children and formed these into a story that explains what we have discovered and what they can do in these often-difficult situations. Stories can help give autistic children, young people and adults a voice. I have even known one or two autistic young people who have written a story to explain to me what they want me to understand. And those are the best stories I've ever read!

Use this book as a guide to help you write your own stories correctly and effectively. As you use and become more confident in using social stories with the child you live or work with, try to involve them and enjoy working it out together. Celebrate their achievements, their personality and their lives alongside providing teaching opportunities and access to new experiences.

References

American Psychological Association (2013). Diagnostic and statistical manual of mental disorder (DSM-5) 5th ed. Washington. American Psychological Association.

Cumine V, Dunlop J & Stevenson J (2010). Autism in the early years: a practical guide. London. Routledge.

Department for Education (2017). Statutory framework for the early years foundation stage: setting the standards for learning, development and care for children from birth to five. London. HMSO.

Frith U (1989). Autism: explaining the enigma. Oxford. Blackwell.

Gray C (2010). The new social story™ book. Arlington, Texas. Future Horizons.

Gray C (2015). The new social story™ book. Arlington, Texas. Future Horizons.

Howley M & Arnold E (2005). Revealing the hidden social code: social stories™ for people with autistic spectrum disorders. London. Jessica Kingsley Publishers.

Lyons V & Fitzgerald M (2013). Atypical sense of self in autism spectrum disorders: a neuro-cognitive perspective. In *Recent Advances in Autism Spectrum Disorders*, 1 (31): 749–770. Intech. https://cdn.intechopen.com/pdfs/41296.pdf

O'Brien T (2015). Inner story: understand your mind. Change your world. CreateSpace Independent Publishing Platform.

Patrick N (2008). Social skills for teens and adults with Apserger Syndrome. London. Jessica Kingsley Publishers.

Toth K, Munson J, Meltzoff A & Dawson G (2006). Early predictors of communication development in young children with autism spectrum disorder: joint attention, imitation, and toy play. In *Journal of Autism and Developmental Disorders*, 36 (8): 993–1005.

Vermeulen P (2013). Autism as context blindness. Shawnee Mission, Kansas. AAPC Publishers.

Vermeulen P (2015). Context blindness in autism spectrum disorder: not using the forest to see the trees as trees. In *Focus on Autism and other Developmental Disabilities*, 30 (3): 182–192. http://journals.sagepub.com/doi/abs/10.1177/1088357614528799

White S, Keonig K & Scahill L (2007). Social skills development in children with autism spectrum disorders: a review of the intervention research. In *Journal of Autism and Developmental Disorders*, 37: 1858–1868. http://static.springer.com/sgw/documents/1379065/application/pdf/Autism3.pdf